Quantum Thoughts

Nicole McCracken

Presentation by *BookLeaf Publishing*

Web: www.bookleafpub.com

E-mail: info@bookleafpub.com

ISBN: 9789358318838

First edition 2023

*Dedicated to God and all the people who
have encouraged me on my writing journey
through the years, especially:*

*My mother for always reading my work and
encouraging me to keep going*

*Mr. Nolan, my 8th and 10th grade English
teacher, for teaching me to love English*

*Germán Hein for listening to my poetry and
helping me write again*

PREFACE

These poems have followed my personal and spiritual journey over the years, written at various points in my life as ways to express my thoughts and the world around me. I've reordered them to create a journey for the reader to explore and delve into the back and forth of life.

Quantum Thoughts

Upon the rosy bed of prose
A soft voice in the night arose
Alight to find this golden den
From here to now to even then
Of words that dance with no refrain
A pleasure to the ear maintain
To tell the tales of love and woe
A place where nothing else can go
The purest form that can express
For not a word used in excess

Welcome Burdened Soul - An Ekphrastic

Painting: Census at Bethlehem by Pieter Bruegel

Cold, bitter, the taste of forbidden myrrh
traversing the path on your tongue
Raking and grinding across the fresh buds meant
to ignite a passion to come
Burning and crackling until your mouth revolts
against its impregnated expense
What sweet, sweet incense
A disguised myth with no value here, this
forgotten truth of poverty's lost wealth
Of broken backs and bending knees, these
shattered bones of brittle ivory
Tired spirits, of not flesh alone, these gold
coated souls far too travel worn
So broken, broken from the scorn
Hear the last caw of the morning rooster's
fleeting, abrasive presence in retreat
Crying out in relief for frankincense poured over
frigid ice of working hearts
The snow eating and absorbing, melting away
from the caustic, healing display
Welcome in bright, morning ray

The Sun in Our Eyes

Hot glowing ball, floating through ethereal waves
So small one's hand can cover it and make it go away
Yet beyond comprehensible in a size so large to
smother the marbles of our tiny universe
It meanders slowly making way for its path, moving
lethargically
And yet, not even the tiniest nanometer does it ever
move from its stationary platform of time and space
It dictates life and existence, and yet seems so
innocent in its bright structure
But a brutal foe is this paradoxical shape, enough to
turn to ash and murder
Life and death lie within its face, too much for mortal
eyes to look upon
But mortality it too dances with, though longer than
the human mind extends
To gift the worlds around, offering light and warmth
beyond the destruction
Good things do not always last, so is its creed
But while they last, it will make a great do for them
to shimmer and shine
And at the end, all must burn, or so it says, trial by
fire
Fire so bright it beckons those brave enough to
venture near
But rise too high and the light will burn, rolling down
the veil of disguise
Until it sets in place where all belongs and none dare
go beyond

Ebb and Flow

White cold water, crashing through my veins
Bursting flames, puncturing through my chest
Painful swirl of fire and ice
No relief
No rest

 Shattering bones without a single fracture
Crumpling under weight that none can see
Yet not a burden on my shoulders
Bending under
Standing over

Determination rising from the pain
Yet apathy tangled in my mind
None can go on from here
I can't
I can

I hurt and yet I feel nothing at all
I feel on the inside nothing small
In the heart and the mind
Travels on
Settles down

Eases away
Comes back

Hope
None

Perhaps
Give in

Ghosts in Time

Time goes on without a thought
It pays us no heed
We follow behind and pick up
Pieces of our dreams
These passing moments with us here
Dance within our mind
Strewn across the path unclear
Trampled and left behind
Breathless wonder what are you?
Friendless, passing foe
Promised us a world of hope
Not Death's darkened blow

Evanescent Heart

In the breeze danced your form
Proud and tall it swayed
In hope I reached out to hear
Your soothing, somber tones

But alas, a spectre cannot speak
Gone to cold, deep soil
This melted heart follows there
To water the cracked stone

 And in everything my gaze beholds
Spirits of your memory
My haunted nose and haunted ears
Strike to remind me

Carved lessons in my soul
Chiseled by your echos
In my being forever dwell
Locked beyond recall

Silent Exulansis

Words cannot describe this
These feelings are not the same
Tears are not always shed
And silence not a symptom
Of wanting... to be alone
How could I make it seen?
This pain inside of me
How am I to explain
Words of so much pain?
I cannot describe
And you cannot hear
I cannot feel it all
I wish I could make sense of this
So you could also see
I'm not me
I'm not who... I used to be
But I'm still not this person
Who I seem to show
Why
Can't you see?
Why can't you understand?
The things I do
The feelings I show...
They're not underhanded
They're just broken
Declarations
Exclamations
Of pain

Artuate

This dark breath exhaled of smoke and ash
Burns with lighted embers through my shattered
chest
Cracking seams along forgotten scars
Glass embed within this turmoiled mind
Reflecting fashes of light and color
Corrupted into images of imagination
A creation of character and design to hide
From the stressed strings tightening 'round
In constriction of the hearts silent cries
Memory and dreams combined to choke
And remind of crashing waves against burning
sand
Explosive pain washed through a typhoon of
blame
Until silence takes the sails and lights the
lanterns
To reveal dysmorphic history realigned to
recreate
This storm settled in wait to pour and rage but
Left to sprinkle in anticipation of a weight too
great
A final blow of this fated pain never meant
For the shoulders of a wounded child's soul

Sandpaper Pain

Swirling dark clouds circle and pull,
Blow tendraled fingers towards my mind
Wispy shadows grasp and grate,
Tangle and pull me further into the depths
Thrashing and turning, this sickening darkness
Begins to engulf spirit and soul
Silent cries echo in thick silence,
Falling short of breath, devoid and broken
Tar and mud coat the throat,
Choking past the understanding and cause
They paint pain, resurfaced to drowning sand,
Grinding grains into emotion, sifting into a
healing heart,
Tearing at old wounds, sanding scars to bleed
Gushed blood in black rain storms and thunders
Into a brain desperate for sleep

Snuffed Spirits - An Ekphrastic

Painting: Transfiguration by Raphael

 The line drawn thin, a sheer curtain between the
epistles
A hand breaks through, reaching up to touch the
rungs of the ladders
Splintered fingers brushed up against holy wood,
clawed of nails trying to grasp
Before it falls, the hole mended as boots climb
upwards, step by step
Feet protected by blessed sandals, eyes cast up to a
blinding light, so bright
Their toes crack against the proximal bonage, crushed
under enlightened weight
The sounds so loud

Snap   Snap
   Crack
Snap   Snap
   Crack
Snap   Snap
   Crack

They merge, regarded as the loud creaks of wood so
used by those ascended
That no one hears the screams of the devastated
souls,
Bitter against the light

Letter to Death

Your fingers are as cold as your gaze, though
I believe I see something deeper, hidden, beyond the seen
Like candles in the dark, lost behind the fabric shrouds
A part of you I've found to love, the spark within your being
You know things seen of the world and the ages
Somewhere
    Somehow
        Someway
Yet I despise you with all the iron pumped through my veins
A warm, burning reminder that thievery in the night suits you
Defines you as the revolting villain behind every tragic story
Like a grave robber in reverse occupation of expectation
To wallow in the painful stretches of time
Waiting
    Lingering
        Watching
Still you astound me, entice me and beckon with a wisdom I seek
Lost questions aching for light to brighten shadows you know
So we speak and you listen, advise, and teach my eyes to open
To see what blindness is better suited for, to consume air
unbreathed
And I become entangled in the snare of grief and acceptance
Stuck
    Caught
        Ensnared
Is this the burden you carry? The night and dark
Shadows your cage? And you, just as much a victim
To the cold, chilling cycle of eternal mortality

Rise Onward

Rise up, stand tall, hear the drums sound
Take a chance, take wing...

Follow

f
o
l
l
o
w

The clouds are high, the winds at ease
This night, this day, and from here we see
We rise up, fall down, we hit the ground
And onward soldier,

Come now...

Come now

One More Day

Take a step, take a breath, lift your arms, let go
Let the darkness rise and wash away
Swirling mist, glowing lights, one more day
One more day, one more breath
Let go, be free, find your place, find your peace
Rain fresh it makes this new
Drops so pure, growing hope pushes through
Pushes through, pushes through
Push me through
Let me breath
Make me free
Take these chains, take these walls, take these
fears
Please ... take it all
One more day to find these hands
To create, to be me
To be me, to be free
If only, Lord help me, I could breathe

Kodiak Kintsugi

Something changes in this vision before my
eyes,
Of the life I have lived and the image in the
mirror I see:
The black and white negatives crumpling from
my past
With pulsating images of sorrow, these Kodiaks
of pain.
All the red rooms, broken dreams, begin to shift
and change
As they roll across the ground, forming
something new.
The haunted thoughts and images once holding
me back,
Tearing and folding as the poisoned ink bleeds
and retracts
Before twisting to combine into this technicolor
sculpture
Like a melted glass Michelangelo stretching
toward my soul -
Molten color pumped into my lungs to grow
inside this glory hole
These hopes and dreams revived again, melting
away

The entangled metallic veins covered in
damaged sheets of bone.
The copper and gold, pressed out from the
cracks of my skin
An alive kintsugi, shattering out brittle and
scarred ribs
Creating images from the traumas in my chest
and broken seams
Of a shattered heart, now coated in creative
dreams
Turning into figures alive in a sudden vision of
words
Thrust forth from the open wound to prove I'm
worth more
Than undefined photos of smeared black and
white,
Or tinted glass blocking out every portion of
light
Or a broken statue barely breathing in monotone
chaos.
But I instead the three-dimensional art of
Picasso and Monet,
Not straight or perfect but a million thoughts
uncontained
Creating a dappled garden of precious metaled
beliefs:
A mural to see, and to touch, and to breathe in
every part,

Splashes of color aligned precariously in this
healing heart.
People think perhaps this is the insane but it's
the image
Of something beautiful and painted into my
landscaped core
Not the thrown-out art of the amateur unwanted
But the priceless masterpiece of the professional
savant.
Because the vision before my eyes is a story
now told
Through art and word, through a personality of
gold:
A broken past made anew into something
beautiful,
An artwork with no boundaries, no set-backs, no
tears.
The shards of history recombined to redefine the
who
And the what of the molded and glued back
together I am:
The beauty of an ancient art, of stained glass, or
better yet
With my words I'm defined to be a collage of
negativity
Reformed with the brushstrokes of colorful
positivity

Life in Dual

Muscle and bone, heart and soul
Two in one and one in the same
Hand dealt, ranks arranged
Cards flipped, Jack of Spades
Armor and facade in masquerade
Scars torn in the dances of pain
Covered faces absorbed the blows
Fingers brushed and broke the mold
Pause
Breathe
A mask of fabric, a helmet of iron
Torn away for naked eyes afraid
A spark lit, fire set ablaze
Flames lick high, born alive
Comfort and trust begin to achieve
A new bond made to set free
To heal and bring forth the new hope
What time and safety will one day show

Discovery Alight - An Ekphrastic

Painting: The Astronomer by Johannes Vermeer

Vibrant light of morning and evening, glowing
to emphasize the conjuring mind
Yellows and oranges, a burst of concept and
thought ablaze on forward tilt
Swirling into a mixture until they glow
radioactive, bubbling and popping
Igniting the world around them in explosions of
grandeur and belief
The word on fire and the people rejoice as the
waves of knowledge sweep
Spinning at hyperdrive, the globe rocking off
course in the weight of ecstasy
As a hand reaches, a palm fitted to the earth to
right the wrongs
Returning the chaos of fitful delight into an
order rightfully on track
To breathe and find the truth sought in the
crevices and heights
The music dying down, the murmurs of the
bland, the yellows ease
Into the cool of the nightly blue and the soft turn
of the sparkling mobile

Designed to Be

Who am I? This is me
My reflection for all to see
Melded to and molded in
Fit to be
This creation made by Thee
Serene and peaceful, His liberty
I am as He made me

Who am I? His to see
This masterpiece of Jubilee
Formed of His image
Thoughtfully made -
Saved through the tree, set free
I am perfect
I am me